How to Win a Hackathon

By Damian Montero
5 Times hackathon winner

Copyright © 2013 Damian Montero

All rights reserved.

ISBN: 1491227311
ISBN-13: 978-1491227312

DEDICATION

This book is dedicated to my beautiful wife, Edilma, which has always pushed me to be a better human being. I also dedicate this to my beautiful daughter, Lily, which has accelerated by love of life by being my guiding light from now to forever.

CONTENTS

1	Introduction	1
2	The Judges	Pg 3
3	The Prizes	Pg 5
4	Your App	Pg 8
5	The Presentation	Pg 11
6	Conclusion	Pg 14
7	About the Author	Pg 15

INTRODUCTION

After wining my 5th consecutive hackathon I sat in my Palm Resort suite in Las Vegas (paid for by my 4th hackathon's winnings) and decided to share my winning tips with everyone.

To start, I want to tell you a story: when visiting the Grand Canyon, we went to an Indian reservation and were privileged to watch a performance by the winning team of the national "Native American Music Contest", these guys have beaten musicians from tribes from all over the Americas. I sat in amazement waiting to be blown away by the winning team that year.

The show started and there it was, what seemed to me at the time, a melody my 2 year old could create without even trying to emulate. This seems not "amazing" but boring. How could THIS be the winning composition? Did they give away these prizes at random?

Had I been lied to? Did all the groups performing any "native American performance" tell you that same story? Were my western ears so sophisticated that this "primitive" music didn't match a little Beethoven or Katy Perry?

Of course not.

They were not the ones that weren't good enough. I was the one that didn't see the subtleties in their performance, what was I missing?
What I lacked was the understanding of WHY THEY could have won their contest.

I had a similar conversation with a very good friend as he tried to explain to me why his "working" app did not win while my not fully complete app came in 3rdplace. He truly wanted to know why. He couldn't see it.
I do not go to these hackathons "hoping" to win. I go into these "concerts" prepared to win and that is what I will be sharing in this book.

I have divided the whole "hackathon" in different winning pieces and I will tell you what to do to nail it: "The Judges", "The Prizes", "Your App" , and "The Presentation".

HOW TO WIN A HACKATHON by Damian Montero

THE JUDGES – THEY'RE HUMAN

These are the individuals that have been chosen to "judge" your app.
The first thing to understand is that they are many things, not just your "judges"

These people are human and so they CAN be "persuade".

There are many things they are looking for, not only the "best app".
I will of course talk about the presentation later, but you must be aware that they're not looking through a list of "things that you must do to win". They are always "judging" whatever you're saying and what your app's possibilities are.

In one hackathon, were I had created an augmented twitter app, one of the judges (a very beautiful blond) came up to me to explain how she couldn't wait until I released this because she could really see herself using it in her car while she drove home.

She had (without my hinting at it) seen a new use for my app which I had never thought of.
That meant that I had won over apps that were more "complete" and maybe more professional looking, because she had remembered my app since she could see herself using it.
So do make yourself "remember-able".

And remember: Be social.

As I mentioned already, these judges are human. Go talk to them. They are not un-touchable (but don't actually TOUCH them...) Before the hackathon if possible, do a little look up in Google and perhaps read their tweeter posts. Get enough "information" to have a small "personalize" chat.

When I won my last hackathon in 2012; I had seen the blackberry judge before (I was learning about blackberry and had seen his posts) and I had read up on what he had talked about in other events. I went up to him and mentioned that I had read his posts, and how I was using what he suggested in my current app. It was a short conversation but he remembered me after that.

Now of course you have to remember. It's social, not a stalker. Don't keep bothering the judges, A quick conversation could help you in the presentation, they may point something important or excuse a service taking longer than you though, or an app crashing in the middle of a presentation.

If "Being social" sounds like something that's "hard for you" remember that you are just going for a small talk, just ask them anything; everybody loves to talk about themselves..

HOW TO WIN A HACKATHON by Damian Montero

THE PRIZES – CHOOSE WISELY

Your app has to cater to the different prizes that are out there. See which one is the prize you want and make sure your app fulfills its requirements or is programmed in the platform or language they want.

My last hackathon of 2012 included different prizes from different companies. There was the standard 1st, 2nd and 3rd which were substantial but not by any means the ones worth the most.

They were cash prizes of $500, $300, and $200 but if you won the "best blackberry app" you could win a trip to "Las Vegas with flight and hotel paid for and a free pass to AT&T's super hackathon where there will be $125,000 worth of prizes" and of course that's what I went for.

We'll talk more about this in the "Your App" Section, but it's important you understand that not all the prizes are compatible, so you first must decide which one is your ultimate goal.

Also see which prizes you have the best chances on. For the blackberry prize I had to develop a BB10 app. This DID mean I might have to learn a new language or platform I was unfamiliar with, but I was already going to have a limited number of competitors (at least at that time) so I spent the prior two weeks becoming a blackberry BB10 expert.

A similar situation happened on that AT&T hackathon in Las Vegas I won.

There was a prize that was provided to the "top 10 windows phone 8 apps" a bag of prizes which added to $3000. That means that all 10 "winners" were going to get this prize.

Now Windows phone 8 (at the moment of this writing) is new and sufficiently different from the more common Android & iOS to make this prize a no brainer. Show up. Make anything truly "acceptable" and you were a shoe in. Your competition was going to be low (and you had to be #1 all the way to #10 and you would win)

Another example of how prizes can be yours for the having is when there's a prize for using a particular service.

When I was on my first hackathon; AT&T offered a $1000 prize "if you use any of AT&T API's ". And they had one API that stood out as the simplest one to use: The SMS API. Simply send a text from your app and you've got the prize.

But don't be surprised to find a lot of times these "extra" prizes are NOT given out because no one used their service. That means that if your app uses these services you may find yourself the automatic winner.

You can win multiple prizes. In my first hackathon my team came in 2nd place overall and won 3 other prizes including one for TeleNav, and the blackberry prize for simply "showing that our app could run on the Blackberry playbook".

Now having said that: make sure you're not "shoe horning it in". That is to say, make sure it kind of makes sense that you're using this service, language or platform. The "sending SMS" is one where you could easily put into ANY app, but just because you can think of HOW you would use it doesn't mean it make sense.

I think that the best test should be "if they DIDN't have a prize for it would you put it in". If the answer is no then either try to think of another way to use it (and maybe another part of the API or service) or simply don't have it. (I don't understand this)

The hackathon is for showing your skills (both technical and social) but if you are there realize that the event is also being held because... you're a wanted commodity.

These hackathons are not about you winning, or feeding you for free. It's a way for companies to get you excited about what they have to offer. And a lot of times they are willing to throw some good cash or prizes at you to achieve this goal.

HOW TO WIN A HACKATHON by Damian Montero

YOUR APP – IT'S WHAT'S ON THE OUTISDE THAT COUNTS

Your app should be a master piece. But of course that's not always possible, not in the time limit they provide. In fact the app most likely will be ugly but the look is the least important thing as long as you have what is in the rules below.

The app MUST be made within the hackathon period and should be made in the location of the hackathon".

This of course said, so that you make an amazing app only to see a goof ball that seemed to be just chatting up a storm , walks up there and presents something that looks like it took 6 months to build.

Now, if you are that goof ball NEVER start the presentation with "today I just added some features to this great app I've been working on for 6 weeks"

Having said that the one thing you DO want to make sure you do test your features to make sure you know you're ready.

HOW TO WIN A HACKATHON by Damian Montero

During my work prior to the hackathon where I won the trip to Las Vegas, I was trying out a "push" feature for my blackberry app. Only to find out that it take 3-6 days to get an "approval" of that service. Well I found this out 3 days BEFORE the hackathon. Luckily (because I tried this ahead of time) the push permissions email came the day before and my app included it. Be prepared to work hard, but have "proof of concept apps" that you can not only use code from, but also where you've knocked out any possible issues (as I did)

- Make it "technically impressive"

Everyone sometimes doesn't read this in most of the descriptions of the hackathons, but it's in there. And If it's not said it's implied.

- Blow some smoke signals:

Always mention what "services" you used. If you can, show a feature that the platform you're developing in wants from its apps before it's "published". For example, if it's a windows 8 app show how the tiles change, or the fact that it integrates with the OS search option.

Convince people that you are a technical wizard in the language or platform you've chosen. You need to wow them not just with your amazing presentation, but with what you've done, and WHY it was easy for you and hard for others.

Showcase something that no one would know unless they saw your code.

When I presented my blackberry app, the blackberry folks wanted to know in what language I had developed it in. I explained not only the language, but why I had selected it, of course showcasing why their platform was the "better one". For me the best prize was the "blackberry" prize in that particulate hackathon and explaining every part of the blackberry platform I had used help me win this prize

Tell the judges what obstacles you have and how you solve them: sound confident, you are the only one who knows what really happen when you were developing the app. Mention how you're using the maps API from Google (It once saved me, because the map took a while to load but in the corner was a tiny logo of Google. This gave me the couple of seconds to explain why I was using it and explaining that it's not always fast) or mention that the information is coming from this great unknown API you found. It makes you sound like you know your stuff.

Point that the backend is written by you today and will be used many many a times because of how versatile it is and how you've learned so much working with it..

HOW TO WIN A HACKATHON by Damian Montero

THE PRESENTATION – TIME TO WOW!

Most of the friends that ask me how is it that in the last 5 hackathon's I've been to so, far I always win one of the big prizes: I always answer: "The presentation my friends"

When I started, not with what the app did but how I presented it, their eyes glance over as if I am joking with them. But I'm not.

Ignoring the presentation or not thinking it's a big deal is a big mistake. Most of the hackathons that have written rules, or explain how you will be "judge", mention not only that your app should be technically impressive, but that a big chunk of the score is how you present it or "the Presentation"

They will usually mention it will be "a third of how they score your app", but it may be more.

I have already talk about how important the judges are and how to improve their perception of you. And yes, they are looking at your app, but the app isn't being submitted and presented by someone else. It's presented by you. And you are being judged along with your idea and your implementation of it in your app.

Here are some simple tricks to follow when presenting:

KEEP TO THE TIME.

You will be given a time. Sometimes there is a big clock somewhere, and sometimes someone's Smartphone keeping track and will tell you only if you get close to the end

But you should keep it short at to the point. And never have it so long that they cut you off. This is the kiss of death.

TELL A STORY

First present your case. Tell a story of what problem you're solving, or of the individual you have built this for. Be brief with this because if you are solving a problem so complex that it will take half the time you have, then you've probably you're explaining details that are obvious.

The problem has to be real and the app you present has to solve that problem.

HAVE YOUR APP READY

Sometimes we want to show the icon or show that you're actually launching the app from your development environment, but usually you can do that at the end. No one will be blown away by your splash screen unless it's going to bring down the house in laughter (and it probably won't)

The last thing you want to have the audience waiting 5-10 seconds as the app loads, or retrieves information.

DON"T JUMP AROUND

You are solving a problem. Make sure to go from step 1 to step 10 in order. You are doing a presentation, not showing your friend this is really a cool app and the last thing you want is to have the judges think YOU were the disorganized one among all the presenters

MIND THE GRAPHICS.

You don't have to be a graphic artist extraordinaire to get great looking apps. There are plenty of free icons, free graphics for inside your apps. And excellent libraries to make your app or website look professional.

INCLUDE THE AUDIENCE

It's always interesting to include the audience. You might not get any volunteers to come up and you might ask a question and find not too many answers, but a little will go a long way. Make sure to look at your judges and maybe ask them a quick question but don't expect an answer. "Does anyone like lunch?" You don't have to wait for an answer but it'll keep some people from talking through your presentation and might wake up some judges that have fallen asleep from your competitors

HOW TO WIN A HACKATHON by Damian Montero

CONCLUSION

In conclusion, these hackathons are not only about the app. You app will be what you show, but what the judges see and what you'll be presenting is yourself. The decisions will be made by regular people that know only what is shown in front of them and how it is presented.

Make me proud and win the best prizes (or at least the ones you REALLY want) cause now you know everything I do.

Good luck.

HOW TO WIN A HACKATHON by Damian Montero

ABOUT THE AUTHOR

Damian Montero is a lifelong programmer with a passion for challenges of any type. Having been a web developer since his first paid job, he wasn't sure that his "mobile app" knowledge. He went to his first hackathon as a way to prove to himself that he was just as good as a mobile app developer as he was as a web developer. Having won 2nd place on that first hackathon proved that he was ready, and lead to this book.

Made in the USA
Middletown, DE
19 December 2016